OUR WARTIME PARISH

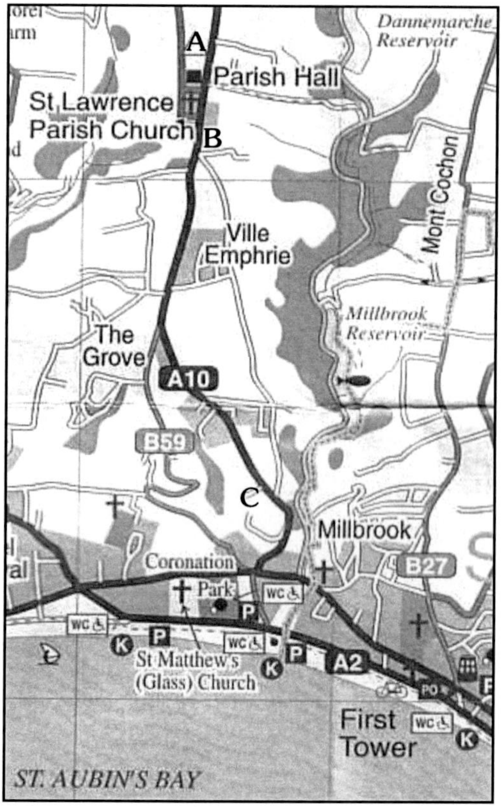

Part of the parish of St Lawrence, Jersey

A St Lawrence School
B Church Lea
C Windycroft

Our Wartime Parish

by

Barbara Journeaux

ELSP

Published in 2013 by ELSP
11 Regents Place
Bradford on Avon
Wiltshire BA15 1ED

www.ex-librisbooks.co.uk

Printed by Orbit Digital Print
Corsham, Wiltshire

ISBN 978-1-906641-56-6

In memory of my parents
and
for my brother and sister

Contents

Mary Ann's the drink for me
Full of kick she used to be
Now alas I rarely see
My dear old Mary Ann

(Sung at the Parish Hall at a concert
In aid of the British Red Cross –
words by HSC)

~ A donation will be made to the British Red Cross from the proceeds of the sale of this book ~

Introduction

My father Harold Shakspeare Carter was born in Clairvale Road, St Helier, Jersey. His parents Harry James and Fanny (*née* Shakspeare) had come to the Island to teach at a small Methodist school in St Ouen and his father later became headmaster of First Tower School.

My father also became headmaster of First Tower School, but was previously headmaster of St Lawrence School during the war years. In 1941 with a postscript in 1945 and following his retirement he wrote several memoirs on different subjects relating to life during the time of the German Occupation of the Island of Jersey, and on re-reading these and before it is too late I thought perhaps they could be combined with my own childhood memories in respect of the village of the Parish of St Lawrence, the surrounding countryside, the School, Parish Hall, Church and the houses in which we lived. The Parish of St Lawrence is one of the twelve Parishes which make up the Channel Island of Jersey.

This is an intimate picture of an ordinary family, father, mother and three small children, Barbara, Nancy and Lawrence, and a little of how it was for the five of us during those years.

In 1940 we were living at a house called Windycroft at the top of Mont Felard, which had been built by my parents in 1932. They bought the land for its construction from my grandfather Philippe Josue Sarre. It overlooked St Aubin's Bay to the southwest and had extensive views over the land to the west. To the south of the house was a property then called Pendeen. On the east side were two fields bisected by a rough track. These fields were used for growing potatoes and tomatoes. The most southerly part of the fields had views over the harbour, Elizabeth Castle and the eastern part of St Aubin's Bay. On the west side of the house was a wild headland with bracken, grass and gorse bushes. Before building commenced a well had to be dug which took a great deal of my parents' savings.

My father took photographs of the German aircraft flying low over Windycroft before the German troops arrived. It was forbidden to take photographs during the Occupation. Fortunately the film survived in his camera hidden for five years and after Liberation Day he was able to take pictures of his three children on the wall beside the Union Jack at Church Lea, the German troops marching past our home on their way to West Park, and of the landing craft waiting to take them to England.

My thanks to Doctor Janet Likeman (*née* Gloyn Ham) for her most welcome, important and major contribution with her fully researched account of education at St Lawrence School during the Occupation years, and for her permission to reproduce the relevant extracts. She was a pupil of my father at St Lawrence School, leaving there in 1953. She had come to live in the Island at the home of her grandparents with her mother after the war. She believes that my father inspired her to eventually undertake a successful academic career.

My thanks also to my sister Nancy, brother Lawrence, daughter-in-law Gillian, Sally Coffin and Damien Horn of The Channel Islands Military Museum, St Ouen's Bay, and to Roger Jones of Seaflower Books who also publishes under the imprint ELSP.

1 Windycroft: Terrible Anxiety

I found an old and well-worn exercise book in my father's papers. When I had read it I realised it was important to record what he had written as a matter of historical interest. The following is a true copy in which he describes vividly the events leading up to the Occupation:

PREFACE

June 20th 1941. I write these notes for whomsoever it may interest in the future, exactly one year after their occurrence, as I again live through mentally these unprecedented days of turmoil.

In the year 1940 the schools had their summer holidays in June, in order that the children might help with the potato crop. Much difficulty was being experienced in shipping the produce owing to difficulty in tonnage available for transport.

Thus I found myself in holidays in June for the first time in my teaching career, being the then head assistant at St Luke's School, the senior department of which had moved to the Jersey Sports Stadium.

The news had been consistently bad, in fact it was so worrying that we decided not to listen for a day or two.

When we did switch on again it was to hear that Paris had fallen and that there had been a change of government in France.

During the latter part of the week ending June 15, Jersey seemed to be the centre of much activity. Bombers and troop carrying aircraft kept arriving and departing in an almost continuous stream, apparently evacuating from Brittany and the Bay of Biscay.

In the Year 1940 the schools had their summer holidays in June, in order that the children might help with the potato crop. Much difficulty was being experienced in shipping the produce, owing to difficulty in tonnage available for transport.

Thus I found myself in holidays in June for the first time in my teaching career, being then head Assistant at St Luke's School, the senior department of which had moved to the Jersey Sports Stadium.

The news had been consistently bad, in fact it was so worrying that we decided not to listen for a day or two.

Sample page from my Father's diary

I was at this period preparing for my Brevet de Capacité exam which was to be held early in July, but with events of such momentous importance seemingly hanging over our heads, swotting was almost out of the question. Early in this week a call had been made for Jersey craft to go to St Malo to help in evacuation should it be necessary. Many small boats went, but their services were not required as most of the personnel were conveyed directly to England. Evacuation was going on from Cherbourg and French Atlantic ports at the same time.

We then heard that Cherbourg had fallen, and for several days the noise of battle from the coast of France could plainly be heard. Spitfires and Hurricanes roared overhead as they came to refuel at the airport on the journey north.

Jersey at this time was to all intents undefended. The militia was guarding strategic points, the Jersey Defence Volunteers were on duty to watch for airborne landings, and the ARP services were functioning, though there were no public shelters available.

On June 7th British army units started arriving in large numbers, bringing the equipment which had been saved from Cherbourg, in the shape of lorries, gun carriers, anti aircraft guns, etc. and the Island immediately began to take on the appearance of a place about to withstand a siege. Curfew was imposed for the first time from 11 p.m. to 6 a.m., sandbags and machine gun nests began to appear and wires were stretched from poles along the Victoria Avenue to prevent planes landing.

Many English residents were in a state of panic, and were doing their utmost to return to England.

As soon as the troops began to arrive and the two large train ferry boats began unloading military supplies I realised we were likely to become the centre of some very severe fighting, and I began to look round for a suitable site for an air raid shelter.

I finally decided to dig it in the shrubbery in the S.W. corner of the garden and commenced excavating a trench 12 ft long, 5 ft wide and 6ft 6 inches deep on the evening of Thursday June 13th. The weather had been fine and hot for weeks and quite unsuited to manual labour of this sort. By bed time I had made good progress, however, and within 24 hours of commencing, the enormous "grave" was dug. Supplies of timber and corrugated iron were already difficult to obtain but were delivered on the 14th, and a friend, Geoffrey Le Gallais whose family lived next door helped me to fix the sides on the Saturday.

Sunday saw the ground being shovelled back on top. Soon after 1 p.m. I received a call to man the ARP post at St Lawrence parish hall as hostile aircraft were presumably about. I dashed off in my old clothes and after waiting there for a couple of hours I returned, nothing having happened.

By Sunday evening the shelter was complete and a general air of insecurity was abroad in the Island.

For the next few days life proceeded more or less normally, everyone waiting for events to shape their destinies. Potatoes were still being dug, and long lines of vans and lorries waited to endeavour to send their loads on the very limited shipping available.

All RAF activity had ceased, and there seemed to be a calm before the storm.

On Monday June 17th it was announced that M. Ragnaud the French prime minister had resigned and that Marshal Petain had taken control and a day later fighting ceased.

On Wednesday June 19th the States met and were informed all British troops were to be withdrawn immediately and the Island was going to be an "open town".

I first heard of this from a workman in the field, as I was going to fetch the *Evening Post* which soon confirmed the report.

It further stated that all men between 20 and 33 were to get to England as speedily as possible, plus all service men on leave, and that arrangements were in hand to evacuate all civilians who desired to leave. These were to be divided into two categories, (a) those who could pay their way and (b) those who could not; and all had to register at the Town Hall in St Helier.

Never had such a blow fallen on the Island, and never before or since have people had to make such a decision as they were faced with that evening.

I immediately tried to get into touch with Mr. Avery, Secretary of the Public Instruction Committee, to see whether anything official was known in regard to civil servants.

The telephone lines were choked, so I got the car out and visited him. He could tell me nothing, so I returned and decided as my native isle did not need me, my duty was plain. I therefore went next door to Pendeen and saw my friend Geoffrey who with Dr. Gordon, a Scottish radiologist, were preparing to leave in order to register. When we arrived soon after 7 p.m. there was a long queue six deep up the Parade nearly as far as Gloucester Street. We waited there without making much progress until 10 p.m. when the crowd was dispersed to get home by the 11 p.m. curfew.

My wife Tony in the meanwhile had been collecting a few of the childen`s belongings to put in a suitcase for the following day.

We discussed plans and preparations in the dining room and began mentally to say farewell to all our household goods. About midnight I went out on to the lawn – a beautiful starlight night and everything seemed at peace – yet who could fortell the morrow?

Thursday June 20th 1940 we were up at 5 a.m. and left Pendeen in Geoffrey`s car at 10 to 6 thus breaking curfew. We were not the sole culprits for when we arrived the queue was almost to Gloucester Street and at least 10 deep again.

Never have I suffered such torture as in that queue. We shuffled forward a few paces each hour and so the morning dragged by. It is still a mystery to me why standing thus causes such acute physical discomfort. By 11 a.m. I was aching in every limb and tried to get relief by crouching, leaning against a shop, sitting on a sill, leaning against one another etc. As we slowly approached the entrance our progress became visibly slower and it was not until later that we discovered that hundreds of people were simply joining the queue at the doors, and protests to the Police were unavailing.

Geoffrey's sister Frances le Gallais brought some refreshment, but I could neither eat nor drink and in this short time her car was stolen by someone anxious to get home and down to the boats. At last we climbed the stairs and registered merely giving our names and address – it was now nearly 3 p.m.

2 Decision to stay

Notices had been posted during the morning that men had to travel on separate boats, and as I waited in that queue I became more and more convinced that in the generally mad conditions prevailing, it would be folly to try to get my wife, just recovering from an operation in April, and three children aged 2, 4 and 6 away. Stories began to gain currency of the appalling conditions under which civilians were to travel, i.e. on coal boats and other cargo vessels without any accommodation whatsoever.

We came home and I met Tony and the children on the lawn and I announced straight away we were not going. Tony was relieved, but Barbara cried bitterly at not going to England. I then sat down to dinner at about 4 p.m. and then sat outside on the terrace and relaxed.

That evening Geoffrey and I went down to the pier to see the conditions of departure. The piers were crowded and barricades were everywhere – boats were leaving at regular intervals, their decks crammed to capacity, and we saw several French officers and sailors on their way to join the free French forces in England.

Next morning I had the unhappy job of taking the Le Gallais to the boat as Geoffrey was joining the Navy as a ship`s officer and Mrs Le Gallais and daughter Frances did not wish to be separated from him if the Island was occupied. The harbours were still crowded and streams of people were still going on board these small cargo vessels. The boat on which they sailed was a regular tramp, at least 40 years old, named the Felspar. She was practically full when they went on board and they had no choice in selecting shelter. Dr. Gordon asked me to go round to his house and hand over his keys to neighbours, then the gangway was removed and the ship sailed. Having completed Dr Gordon's jobs I returned home and we started clearing up the Le Gallais house Pendeen.

The scenes on the pier were incredible. Hundreds of cars were abandoned or given away. Children got lost or separated from their parents, in fact the whole Island was in a panic. This had been almost entirely due to the way the business was handled by the States, and the report in the Evening Post of Wednesday which gave no guide or lead to the people. During Wednesday night there was a council of war in every house, relatives sought advice from each other and decisions were made and changed hourly. During our wait in the queue we were addressed by the Bailiff and by Jurat Dorey who had just returned by RAF bomber after consultation with Home Office authorities.

Both urged the natives to stay and said this was the wish of the British Government who were already in difficulties with large numbers of refugees from the Continent. That evening many people who were intending leaving the next morning changed their minds on reading the reports and these speeches, and further deliberations by the States. It was also stated that all civil servants were to stay at their posts.

The handling of the whole affair had been disgusting, particularly the registration. Many old people collapsed in the queue which was quite unnecessary, for the next day a small typewritten notice was pinned to the door of the Town Hall which read "NO NEED TO REGISTER – PROCEED STRAIGHT TO THE BOAT"! The last evacuation ship sailed at about midday on Friday 21st and the Island began slowly to settle down again from the shock and stress.

I took the opportunity in the afternoon of writing to my relatives in Dudley explaining our position and taking the opportunity of wishing them a happy Xmas as I felt convinced we should soon be cut off from England. In the next day or so we had letters from our relatives the Murrays and the Carters offering us refuge, but we never replied.

On Saturday afternoon I took Le Gallais' luggage to the pier and got it dispatched to Muirkirk, Ayreshire, the home of Dr Gordon whose car I returned to the garage at the same time. Geoffrey`s calling up papers came and were redirected in time, and so all the jobs attendant on this very tragic episode were cleared up, and we were again left to await events. Horses, cows, poultry and rabbits were cast adrift in fields. At the junction of Felard and Cambrai a house was given to the gardener.

We who remained realised our occupation by the Germans was imminent and started making what plans we could to avoid starvation. Le Gallais left us the produce in their garden and Tony proceeded to make jam. I planted several rows of beans for winter use and transplanted winter cabbages, cauliflowers, leeks, and onions in a strip of the field next to the house.

Monday June 23rd saw the first German planes flying backwards and forwards very high. It was only with my telescope that I could see the black crosses painted under the wings. From then on they came daily, flying lower and lower, and once or twice swooping low over the harbour and opening fire with machine guns. On Friday June 28th we had to go to town and I was appalled at the lines of lorries and vans loaded with potatoes stretching past Mont Felard waiting to sell their produce. Here indeed was a target for aerial attack! During the afternoon – a perfect summer's day – we heard several loud explosions to the northwest of the Island.

Just before 7 p.m. we were sitting on the terrace, Nancy and Lawrence being asleep in bed and Barbara was erecting an ingenious device with a small toy white enamel teapot to water her flowers in the back garden. Suddenly the calm was shattered by a terrific explosion from town. Barbara came dashing round the corner of the loggia and I told Tony to get straight to the air raid shelter. I dashed upstairs and managed to get Nancy over one

German Junkers JU52 transport aircraft

The same aircraft flying low with the greenhouse at Windycroft in foreground

German Dornier reconaissance aircraft 17Z from Staffel Aufklarungsgruppe (f) 1234UMK

Same aircraft over St Aubin's Bay; St Matthew's Church and St Aubin's Fort visible in background

shoulder and Lawrence over the other and so carried them across the lawn. As I came out of the front door I could see three planes circling round and machine gunning the town. I was amazed by the huge column of smoke which was already ascending from the piers. After a few minutes the air raid alarm wailed. The children were quite comfortable and not unduly alarmed. The main attack had been delivered at that first blow but the planes kept circling round machine gunning continuously.

I stood at the pillars of the driveway and only when the planes came towards me did I join the others and closed the "lid". About this time a fourth plane approached from the northwest accompanied by the sound of gunfire. We heard the explosions of bombs in the shelter as it arrived over town. Just before 8 p.m. after all had been quiet for some time we emerged, put the children to bed and heard the all clear as we were having a cup of tea. During the 9 o'clock news it was announced that Jersey and the other Channel Islands had been evacuated and we were now open towns.

I was fetched out of bed about 11 p.m. and told to man the A.R.P. post. I left all the family in bed hoping for the best and went in my car to the Parish Hall. When I got there I was informed that orders were cancelled (the midnight news announced a severe raid).

I proceeded to town on my bicycle the following day and as I was in Broad Street the sirens went again. I cycled back and proceeded to the Parish Hall, sighting the plane on my journey as it flew low over St. Aubin's Bay. A few rounds were fired into the smouldering remains of Norman`s Store and the heath fire on Fort Regent. Planes were over again on Sunday when the alarm went just over dinner. This plane circled low over the Airport apparently taking photographs.

On Monday I heard a message had been dropped informing the Bailiff that the Island was to be occupied on the following day, and white crosses were to be painted in the Royal Square, at the top of the Harbour and at the Airport, besides which a white flag was to be flown from all houses in token surrender. This was confirmed later by posters all over the Island. Apprehension filled our hearts.

Thus ended my father's account of events leading to the occupation of the Island in June, 1940 which he wrote in 1941 while his memory was still fresh, and there is a postscript to this document which was written on the back cover of the exercise book headed 'Forty years later' and to which I will refer later.

My own memories of the bombardment are such that I can still point to the spot where I had my tiny garden which I was watering when there was the terrible sound of bombs . I can remember my mother running across the lawn to the air raid shelter carrying the bedclothes of my sister and brother, and, although he seems not to have remembered, my father took me to see the bombs dropping before we rushed into the shelter.

In his desk drawer I found an old piece of paper which contained a message from the King and which was read in the States on 24th June 1940 and which it was alleged that the *Press* had been forbidden to publish. The message reads as follows:

> **Message from the King to the Bailiffs of Jersey and Guernsey**
>
> For strategic reasons it has been found necessary to withdraw the armed forces from the Channel Islands. I deeply regret this necessity and I wish to assure my people in the Islands that in taking this decision my Government have not been unmindful of their position. It is in their interest that this step should be taken in present circumstances. The long associations of the Islands with the Crown and the loyal service the people of the Islands have rendered to my ancestors and myself are guarantees that the link between us will remain unbroken, and I know that my people in the Islands will look forward with the

same confidence as I do to the day when the resolute fortitude with which we face our present difficulties will reap the reward of victory.

3 *We are occupied*

The German troops arrived and set about their task of fortifying the Island and settling in. My father tells the story of his bad experience with a cow, he writes:

> Realising at the beginning of the Occupation that there would eventually be extreme shortages I decided to buy a real live Jersey cow to provide daily sustenance for my children. What trouble it caused, making a stable, learning to milk, running short of pasture, making hay which went mouldy and finally having to make an appearance before the Royal Court. The charge was that I was keeping all the milk for my family and not sending a proportion to the dairy, which was also supplying the German troops. The Bailiff ordered that the cow should be confiscated and I was fined £20.

I remember that as the occupation progressed the house next door, Pendeen, formerly inhabited by the Le Gallais family and previously referred to, was soon taken over by the German military as accommodation for the ever increasing number of troops. I can remember the sound of stamping horses in the converted garage. Fortifications were built, including slit trenches all around the west side of our house, gun emplacements in the lower field and three bunkers nearby. My mother noticed that one of the trenches dug for telephone wires was about to go through her rhubarb patch and she complained. The trench was re-routed. We became accustomed to German soldiers being around the house and garden and in the fields.

After the War my father read the Occupation Diary written by Baron Hans Max von Aufsess who was a Commandant of the Island and wrote a personal letter to him about his experiences with the officers who lived at Pendeen, part of which is as follows:

> One of our neighbours was Lieutenant Zievecka (?) of Hamburg. He was convinced Germany could not be beaten and informed me that the Channel Isles would permanently remain German territory. He asked me if I was learning his language, my reply being in the negative. I asked him what would happen to me at the end of the war, and I was told I would find employment at the Pomme d'Or Hotel as this was to become a Strength through Joy Island. He was not so full of himself after the British bombers had caused a fire storm in Hamburg. He once invited himself to my house to share a bottle of wine which he provided, but I drank very little as I feared my tongue might have been loosened and I would have revealed my innermost thoughts on him and his gang. There appeared daily in the newspaper The Evening Post 'verboten this and verboten that' (forbidden). Naturally it was the preoccupation of the civil population either to ignore, defy or circumvent these orders.
>
> Among the twenty or so soldiers living there, a Lieutenant Engler also had his quarters. At that time my children were aged three, five and seven, and he made friends with them. As I got to know him, I learnt he was a sculptor from Erfurt and we had many discussions of topical interest. Even in 1942 I was bold enough to tell him that Germany was certain to be beaten eventually. In October 1942 the military administration requisitioned my house and I had seven days to find elsewhere to live. I still vividly remember I was shovelling the remains of my coal into bags when he came across to say how sorry he was at our having to leave. Some months later he traced me to our temporary residence. He came to inform me that he had been transferred to the Russian front and I felt our prognostications were alike.

Some weeks after a soldier, whom I did not know, stopped me to say he had been killed. Soon after the liberation we received a letter from his widow describing how he had given her instructions to get in touch with us if she was lacking in food stuffs and clothes. We sent several parcels until she announced she had remarried."

My own memory of Officer Engler, as he was known to us, was of an extremely handsome man decked in splendid uniform riding an equally well groomed horse. Amazingly, when alterations were made to my parents` home at a much later date a photo of him was found at the back of a closed up fireplace.

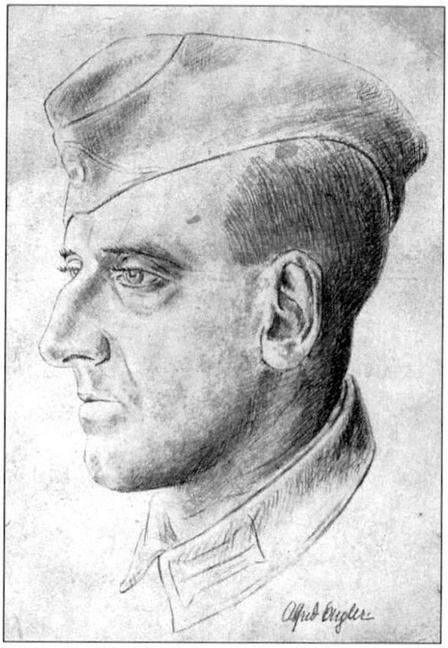

The requisition order received by my father is still in the family and reads:

STANDORTKOMMANDANTUR DEN 24.10.42

JERSEY

Requisition order for "Windycroft", Mont Felard

"Windycroft", Mont Felard, is required by the German forces and hereby requisitioned. The house must be vacated within 8 days time; all furniture may be removed, but all blackouts must remain in the house.

Owner: Mr Carter Standortkommandantur

(signature illegible) Standortoffizier

4 Church Lea

My sister brother and myself were sent to stay with our Aunt Gwenda and Uncle Bill who lived nearby at Clifton in Rue de Bas while the move took place to Church Lea, a pretty house close to the Church and which is currently known as the Villa Doro Guest House. The house was already occupied by an older lady called Miss Le Sueur who had her own quarters. The only sources of heat were small fire places in the living/dining room and one of the bedrooms and the gas cooker in the kitchen. There was a good walled garden at the back where we kept rabbits and chickens. At that time I was not tall enough to see over the wall in front of the house which is now the churchyard. Next door, at Plaisance, lived two older ladies who were caring for two boys called, I believe, Charlie Bree and Richard Fontaine. We would meet up on top of the party wall and they became friends, especially of my brother. I do not know what became of them. Next door to the north lived an Italian family, good neighbours, whose son Emilio was also a friend of my brother. I believe my mother often gave them food. We were all pupils at St Lawrence school, a short walk away, where my father was headmaster.

My mother was born at Le Pont, St John, the fourth of five children. Her parents were Philippe Josue Sarre and Lydia (*née* Vaudin). She was tiny and very pretty. She spoke Jersey French before she spoke French, then English. Before her marriage she taught French in England and in Jersey. She was an excellent housekeeper and cook and gave us as good meals as was possible since she had learned from her mother how to make the best of everything. Although she and my father became very thin I do not remember feeling hungry.

The local farmers were very generous towards us, and it was my job to secretly collect a small churn of milk from the Caurel's farm in Rue de Bas. One day as I was returning home a German soldier stepped out in front of me and put his hand up for me to stop which was very frightening as I knew I must not do so. Instead I gave him a daffodil from the bunch in the basket strapped to my handlebars which was hiding the milk churn. He seemed surprised so I cycled round him as fast as I could.

As we ran out of fuel it became the job of the children to collect firewood which we did mainly by dropping down into Waterworks Valley through tracks and farmland and wood was gathered from the western slopes and carried up to where we had left our cart which had been made by my father. This cart was a very important part of our lives, and my father writes:

> To provide a mobile receptacle, the old family pram was taken apart by myself to provide the four wheels – the rear axle was static but the front was mobile and attached to a long handle which provided the necessary steerage. Apart from its utilitarian aspect it was a most splendid source of entertainment for the young family, for, sitting in the box, they were able to guide the contraption with cord attached to the handle when travelling at considerable speed down Rue de Bas and other suitable gradients. My five year old son also used it aided by his Italian friend Emilio, an ally of the Germans, to steal suitable lengths of tree trunks cut down by the soldiers which I hid in a tall bed of nettles in the corner of the garden.

I will always remember that cart and the hours of enjoyment it gave us. There was always a challenge to see how far down the Rue de Bas we could get starting at Plaisance from a running start, pushing then jumping in.

My sister, brother and I once had to deliver a large wooden wind up gramophone to my Uncle Phil's house at Bel Royal and we decided to go down Mont Cambrai. At the hairpin bend we looked up to see Windycroft and wondered how things were there. It was quite hard to hold the cart back on the steep bits but when we came to the lower part of the hill we decided we could all jump in and ride and see how far we could get. As the eldest and biggest, I held the two pieces of cord controlling the steering and my brother and my sister held the cart steady before also jumping in. Unfortunately the gradient was steeper than we thought, and with the extra weight of the gramophone, the cart took off at speed. My sister recalls that I shouted at her to get out in the hope that she could somehow slow it down, but unfortunately in doing so she fell flat on her face in the road, leaving my brother and myself in the cart, racing down the slope and rounding the corner towards Bel Royal on two wheels. It was a miracle it did not overturn. My sister ran to see what had happened, fearing the worst. This episode still makes me laugh.

As the eldest of his children it was my job to help my father cut up the larger bits of wood. He had constructed a sawing horse in the disused garage in which the wood was stored and I had to hold one end of the big cross-cut saw, which is still in existence. I also became proficient at chopping kindling wood with my father`s billhook, which I still use. Many hours were spent in this way and I still feel I have to pick up bits of twigs. As gas supplies became unreliable my mother, and doubtless everyone else, took advantage of the times it was available and my father describes how they were able to feed us using another method:

> The other invaluable piece of construction was the hay box. The exterior was constructed of plywood with an interior lining of insulation and made large enough to take two saucepans
>
> Having put these in place, and always using the same two, a quantity of hay was forced into all the vacant space, making two nests with a form of

mattress resting on top and pressed down by the tightly fitting lid. The contents of the saucepans had to be boiled fiercely before insertion and they then simmered gently for hours. Although the house was very ancient there was no old fashioned Jersey grate on which to cook. Fortunately in an adjoining outhouse there was a wide open fireplace where a fire was lit early in the morning and the porridge ration which had been simmering all night, was prepared. To this was added milk and sugar beet syrup. With the embers still smouldering, the fire was rekindled and the midday meal prepared.

5 *Hungry Soldiers*

Towards the end of the Occupation food could no longer be shipped in from France and the occupying forces became increasingly hungry. I recall that due to the likelihood of German soldiers breaking into our home it was necessary to carry all items of food upstairs. I had to help my father put the chickens into a loft each night and was once awoken by my father trying to kill a mouse which had run over my mother while she slept by hitting it with his slipper. The mouse was after the flour and other food which was stored in a cupboard in their bedroom.

The isolated Rectory across the field was often broken into and eventually it was suggested that the Rector should blow a whistle from an upstairs window when this took place, and those of the villagers who heard it would open their windows and shout. There was a rumour that the soldiers were eating cats and dogs, and we were anxious about our cat Judy.

One evening I was outside as dusk fell and looked up to see a

German soldier peering over the back wall. I told my father and, shortly thereafter, heard noises in the night and looked out of my bedroom window which was at the back of the house. I could see the outline of German soldiers below, trying to get inside. I woke my father who quickly opened my bedroom window and shouted at them and pelted them with old batteries put there expressly for that purpose. They ran away over the wall as our gate was securely locked.

6 *Slave Workers and Prisoners of War*

One day I was sent on my bike to fetch something from Hibbs, the grocer at Millbrook, but was stopped by soldiers at the barbed wire tank barrier a few yards from the bottom of Mont Felard. A column of Russian and other prisoners of war walked slowly past, with heads bowed, filthy and in rags. I was deeply shocked and will never forget their despair and suffering.

My father also describes seeing these Russians and writes:

> "I was cycling into town to change books at Boots` library and in the distance near West Park I became aware of a strange apparition. I realised it was a human slave gang guarded by German soldiers. Such a pathetic group of humanity would normally be beyond one`s wildest imagination. They had just been landed at the harbour and were walking to one of the Todt slave camps. They were in Jersey to work and possibly die to fulfil Hitler`s design that the Island should become an unassailable fortress. Their slow progress could only be described as a shuffle. Their appearance defied description, they must have walked far for they had no boots and their feet were bound up with sacking. Interspersed within the group

was a small number of women and children. I saw one of these boys at Liberation time. He had obviously been adopted as a regimental mascot for he was wearing an immaculate uniform and was a small replica of a German soldier.

My father continues:

Halfway down Ville Emphrie lived a handyman named André and on my way to visit him I noticed several slave labourers shambling up the hill carrying churns to get drinking water from the well. As the guard had not appeared round the curve in the road I quickly got some cigarettes from my tin and put them on the stonework. As they passed I pointed and mimed the action of smoking a cigarette. When they returned with full cans en route for the underground hospital excavation they surreptitiously acknowledged receipt of them with thanks. It was a foolish spontaneous action as two of my friends had previously been sent to a French prison on the outskirts of Paris for trying to communicate news of Russian victories through the barbed wire of their encampment.

For several months Peter, an escaped Russian prisoner of war, would appear each morning for breakfast after a night spent in some hideout in Waterworks Valley. He would spend the morning in the kitchen looking at the children`s books and learning English with their help. He had his dinner at another house. He was also helped a great deal by my brother in law Bill Sarre

He had discovered that an organisation in St. Helier was prepared to supply him with false identity papers but it was necessary to have his hair style changed for a photograph. I walked with him for a mile or so to visit Mr Le Gros, the hairdresser at Millbrook. We had to pass at least three German encampments and I took my bicycle with me to ensure a quick getaway if necessary. I explained to the hairdresser that he was deaf and dumb and wanted his hair cut short with a parting in the middle. While this was being done two soldiers entered and sat either side of me. Thus did he survive and avoid recapture, and we were equally fortunate to escape detection for what in German eyes, was a most serious crime. That was the last we saw of Peter. He was never recaptured and was repatriated in 1945. His fate thereafter is unknown.

My memory of him which my father seems to have forgotten is that one night after curfew the doorbell rang repeatedly and there was also a loud banging on the front door. We were all in bed, woke up and stood on the landing feeling very alarmed. My father went down to see who was there. Peter fell into the hall and said he was being chased by the German soldiers and needed a bicycle and some shoes. My father could not give him a bicycle, but I remember he gave him some white tennis shoes. Peter then disappeared into the night. We all knew very well not to tell anyone about this.

Whilst on our wooding forays in Waterworks Valley we came across an empty house which stood on the east side of the valley opposite the land which now belongs to the Domaine des Vaux. We found a hidden and well worn path and got in through a window and explored. When we were on the top floor in one of the rooms we heard a sound of loud footsteps on the stairs and someone running away. We were shocked and frightened and got out as fast as we could. Once outside there was no one to be seen, and we assumed it must have been an escaped prisoner of war hiding there, perhaps it was Peter. How he was not found by the German soldiers is a mystery.

My mother and children at Windycroft, 1941/2

My father and children in back garden at Church Lea following Liberation. The children have grown but my father looks thin

7 *Betrayal*

My father writes about a matter which upset him deeply:

> It astonished me that some local residents could betray their own people. Many were saved by the Post Office sorters who withheld the letters, and warned the intended victims of impending danger.
>
> One such betrayal concerns Louise Gould who kept a small grocery shop at St Ouen. She got news that her only son had lost his life in an Atlantic convoy, so when a young Russian begged for help she virtually adopted him as a replacement for her lost son. Someone told the authorities and not long afterwards her house was searched by the Field Police and the escapee and a wireless were found. She had to face a local Military Court, was sent to prison in Fresnes, Paris, and ended up at Ravensbruck where she died, possibly in the gas chambers.
>
> An even greater injustice concerns my teacher colleague Harold le Druillenec who was the brother of Mrs. Gould. The Field Police came to question him whether he knew a Russian was being sheltered by his sister. He readily admitted seeing him several times. Asked why he had not reported this "crime" he replied that it was a recognised British tradition not to "sneak" on others. The Military Court found him guilty of being an accessory and he also was sent to prison in France. Later he was transferred to the shipyards of Willemshaven where he became a welder on submarines. He was a big broad man, almost a heavy weight but the combination of hard work and poor food caused a rapid deterioration in his physique. When he could no longer do the job and thus became useless to his Nazi taskmasters, he was sent to Belsen where I understand he had to

assist in putting bodies into the incinerators. The camp was liberated in the nick of time by the British, for he was suffering from typhus, was virtually a skeleton, and was covered with lice. He was flown to England and his life was saved by the newly found drug penicillin. He was in hospital for months and came back to Jersey with a pronounced limp.

He was the only British survivor of Belsen and was taken to Nurenburg to give a firsthand account of his sufferings at the trial of the Nazi criminals. After a year or so he resumed teaching to become headmaster of St John`s School. I attended his funeral. In essence this was why the last war had to be fought – to eliminate dictatorship and brutality from the face of the earth.

8 How we lived

My father explains how we survived from day to day, and writes:

It was amazing how we Islanders overcame the many difficulties and shortages which were constantly with us. How new ingredients became part of our daily diet – potato flour, sugar beet syrup, a jelly from seaweed and sea water in which to boil our vegetables. Crystal sets were produced by the thousand – I still have mine, and it is greatly treasured for the sound of the voice of Winston Churchill coming through loud and clear on May 8th. The cobbler in Ville Emphrie mended the children's shoes with pieces of the side walls of motor tyres and when the uppers were beyond repair wooden clogs with straps were produced. A column in the Evening Post was full of offers of items for exchange, one of which said `a bedpan for what?' When the German troops arrived they were astonished by the cleanliness of the Island and by the huge stocks in the shops. For years they had been exhorted by the slogan 'Guns before butter' so they quickly descended on the plentitude available.

I remember that my mother knitted endlessly, unravelling wool from other garments and our socks and mittens were marvellous with perfectly turned heels and thumbs. I believe she used four pointed needles which I still have. Our slippers were these socks with old rubber hot water bottle cut out for soles. Miss Downer who lived in Rue Verte made dresses from curtains and everyone wore clothes which had been handed down from older children, people who had left the Island or the deceased. Fashion and vanity did not exist, and as our hair was cut by Mr Le Gros the men`s hairdresser at Millbrook the girls usually looked like boys. My mother wore mens` underclothes, and my father wore an ancient brown wool balaclava hat in cold weather, inside and out.

There were two wood fires in the house, one for Miss Le Sueur and one for us in the dining/living room and sometimes a fire was lit in the upstairs bedroom if we were ill. My father provided wood for Miss Le Sueur. The rest of the house was bitterly cold in winter and if there was no hot water to fill the stone hot water bed warmers we got into very cold beds. I can remember my father telling my mother that he had not washed the children before they went to bed as it was too cold. We had green soap from a tin which was also used to wash our hair. We never had a new toothbrush and probably no toothpaste. Frost often made lovely patterns inside our windows.

One day my sister, friend Kathleen and I decided to play in the field opposite the Parish Hall, bordering on Mont Misère. Suddenly an Allied small aircraft appeared from the west behind the Parish Hall, flying low. We could see flashing lights coming from the cockpit, and presumably it had been taking photos of the airport. At once the German guns opened up from the east side of Waterworks

Valley and puffs of smoke appeared around the plane and shrapnel started to screech and fall around us. We ran into the hawthorn hedge at the side of the hill for shelter and when all was quiet found red hot shrapnel in the field which could have killed us.

My cousin tells me that when an Allied plane came over and the guns opened up she and her sister used to run into their garden at Bel Royal and shout "missed! missed!"

Towards the end of the war our sleep was often disturbed by the droning noise of large numbers of Allied aircraft flying over the Island and the German guns firing. Sometimes the soldiers had mock battles which went on all night and sleep was impossible due to the sound of rifle fire. However the next day we added to our collection of empty ammunition shells and it was always our hope that we would find some live ones.

Far louder and more frightening than the German guns was a terrible thunderstorm which hit the Parish one day. We all crouched beneath the dining room table, and a nearby tree was struck by lightning. We later had a look at the tree which was blackened and smelled of fire.

My father described what life was like for him personally:

> The German Reichmark, specially printed for use in the occupied countries, was not worth the paper it was printed on except as the then legal tender for the minimal rations provided. Richness in those five years depended entirely on what goods you possessed or on foods which were produced. I had little with which to barter and remember coming home one day to be told by my wife that she had just swopped my dress suit for a bag of corn. Having been evicted from my house and productive garden by the Germans in 1942 I found I had some spare time which I spent on the farm of the late Charles Poignard at Les Ormes helping with routine jobs, my reward being a Mary Ann bottle filled with milk for my children.

Before the war the States farm with miraculous foresight had obtained seed of the best Virginian tobacco for experimental purposes. As a smoker I often used my meagre ration too early in the week. In Spring 1944 my farmer friend obtained about 200 tobacco plants. The dilemma was where to grow them to prevent them being stolen but my friend`s solution was instant and obvious. Where better than guarded by German sentries day and night? Adjacent to his farm and across the lane was a huge German artillery encampment with about twenty French 'seventy fives' well dug in. He was still permitted to use the remainder of the field to graze his cattle and I was never challenged when I accompanied him to move them. Thus in the middle of the field he ploughed a strip and the tobacco was planted. Whether it was the stable manure, the climate or my careful tending I do not know, but they thrived, growing to over five feet tall. The harvest began towards the end of the summer. As the lowest leaves turned yellow they were plucked and carried up to a loft in the outbuildings where they were placed in piles about nine inches high and allowed to sweat for about ten days until the leaves became golden. These were then strung on long wires like washing under the rafters where they dried to perfection. We eventually had about 150 pounds of tobacco, which we shared.

A cigarette factory was still in operation in St. Helier where we took a bundle of leaves for cutting, and collected an equal weight the following week to be rolled in our Ritzla machines. I was able to provide tobacco for bartering for sugar beet syrup or potato flour, my wife being in charge of the delicate negotiations.

For several months I went back and forth through the German gun positions. Just after the surrender and before the prisoners were shipped to England the German sergeant said these words to my farmer friend `if there had been an Allied landing in Jersey, the big Englishman was going to be the first one shot because of his knowledge of our encampment.

While my father was engaged in growing tobacco and other vital activities connected with our survival we, the gang of children, and sadly I am unable to remember who they all were, often occupied ourselves by exploring a hidden valley which was situated at the bottom of the Perquage or sanctuary path which began at the west door of St Lawrence Church. This valley was seldom frequented by the German soldiers and the perfect place to create paddling pools in the brook since we were unable to go on the beach, search for eels and make camps in the holm oak trees from which we could observe any soldiers who happened to pass by. They never saw us as we were all alert to any unusual sounds and very aware of the dangers which could arise.

One winter there was a snowfall which was unfortunate for us as we could not stay out long due to our thin clothes, but my young brother entering into the spirit of throwing snowballs threw one at a German officer passing by in the road from one of the upstairs windows of Church Lea. Unfortunately it hit his dagger and caused the officer to have a furious rage and his shouting at my brother was terrifying to hear.

We had a wonderful playground in the road opposite the house which was empty for most of the time, and where we could play ball, hopscotch, skip, make shapes in the melting tar in summer time and generally mess about. Sometimes a squad of soldiers would march past singing the song which began aye ee aye oh aye oh and sometimes a large covered wagon would appear pulled by great horses, taking supplies to the encampments to the north of us.

If we were ill we went to bed until we recovered. If we were very ill it was an important occasion, the bedclothes were changed, and the doctor was called. He gave us some tablets called I believe, M + B, which seemed to make us worse. However my mother made the most wonderful chicken broth to aid our recovery. She cooked a proper stock from a chicken carcass, and having strained this added finely grated carrot, shredded cabbage, chopped potato and if available, peas. On the surface floated golden droplets of fat.

A fire was lit in an upstairs bedroom, and the warm ashes often attracted mice who were probably as cold as we were. When all the rubber hot water bottles had perished and become soles for slippers we used the old fashioned stone hot water bed warmer which was moved from bed to bed to warm it up a bit before the occupant arrived, and I recall being unable to put my feet down to the bottom of the bed it was so cold. When we were ill we were especially glad of the childrens` books my father collected for us every Saturday morning on his bike from the junior library in Dumaresq Street.

While they were small enough my father carried my sister on the crowbar of his bike and my brother on the carrier. I pedalled hard on a too small child`s bike and was very glad to have it. When I grew out of it I shared my mother`s bike and the small bike went to my sister.

In the summer, the early morning sun came into my bedroom and sometimes I could hear the clinking of harness and the farmer talking to his horse as he ploughed the field behind the house.

We were completely cut off from the outside world, and my father writes:

> Our cameras and radios had been confiscated and our sole contact with the outside world was a single sheet of newsprint containing the official German war communiqué, plus the repeated use of the word 'verboten' (forbidden). Of great interest was column after column of 'exchange and mart'. The paper money printed by the Germans was virtually useless as there was little to buy, unless it was highly priced black market goods. In 1942 I paid £10 for one pound of tea! However some refused to conform and secreted their radio sets, and so the news was disseminated – with first a good look over the shoulder! My 'broadsheet' was delivered twice weekly by the baker with his horse and two wheeler. Thank you Charlie le Sueur.

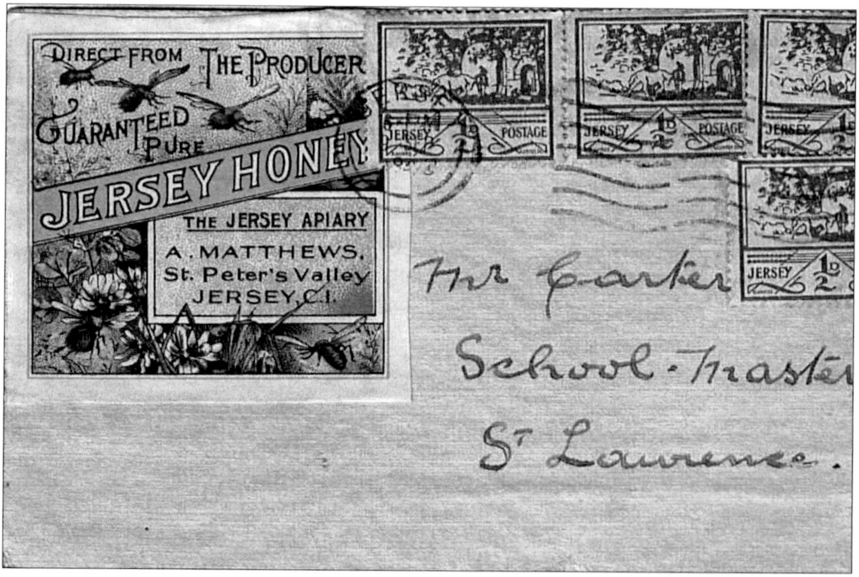

Letters addressed to Father during the Occupation

9 St Lawrence Elementary School

St Lawrence Elementary School, a fine pink granite building, is situated to the north of the Arsenal and on the St Lawrence main road. The back entrance is on a narrow lane leading down into the rural heart of the Parish. The boys' entrance, cloakroom and yard were on the east side and the girls' on the west. The children lined up to go into school at their appropriate entrances. There were two classrooms on the north side together with a small staffroom and cloakroom, to the west was the infants' room and to the south was the top class and the soup room which were divided by a wooden sliding partition. To the southwest there was a rough playing field. Part of this later became the air raid shelter, a damp and unpleasant place lined with timber and fungi. The lavatories were in the respective yards into which they opened directly, and if I remember correctly were called "the backs". In wintertime it was necessary to take a coat when visiting. I never went into the Boys' Yard.

My father writes:

In September, 1940 the Headmaster of St Lawrence`s School died suddenly and I was appointed to succeed him. What had I inherited? Approximately one hundred boys and girls aged six to fourteen, a staff of three, two of whom were unqualified, and a deplorable lack of books and equipment. Here were both challenge and responsibility. Come what may these children must acquire a sound basic education, so that when hostilities ceased, they would be fully equipped to proceed to higher education.

Further, should the war be lost, they should also have acquired a sound basic knowledge of English literature, poetry, and above all patriotic songs. In this latter aim I was assisted by an elderly lady pianist, Miss Luce, a piano which had never been tuned, and above all a splendid song book by Murdoch. It was wonderful to hear the lusty singing of *Rule Britannia,* and the British Grenadiers as the German Feldwebel drilled his squad on the adjacent playing field. We had a second music session during the week – this time devoted to hymn singing, and we invariably finished with the same tune, *God Save the King.*

It had become impossible for my father to get me to the preparatory department of what was then known as the Ladies' College and after a short while at First Tower School I was sent to St Lawrence Elementary School where my father had recently become headmaster, and was put into a class of mixed boys and girls which was strictly controlled by a devoted teacher named, I believe, Miss Laurens. She was handy with the ruler and accurate with the blackboard cleaner which was necessary. She had a very sharp tongue. I then moved up to Miss Blacklin`s class, another devoted teacher who cycled to school every day from her home in St Saviour's Road. In this class, while the boys were taken out to do something probably more interesting, the girls were taught to sew and embroider, and usefully how to patch and darn.

My last class was the top class, taught by my father. His large desk was on a dais. In the bottom right hand drawer he kept his cane, and when the occasion demanded the class except for the bad boy was sent into the corridor. He had the gift of removing the cane from its drawer and slamming it onto his desk with one smooth movement whenever the class threatened to get even slightly out of control. Without thinking I once went home one break time to fetch something I had forgotten and my father made me write a hundred lines as punishment.

I, Constable of the Parish of St Lawrence
certify that the holder of this card, namely,
resides at
in the said Parish.
1940.
Constable
Chef de Police
Signature of Holder (a)
(a) To be signed on issue.
J. T. Bigwood Ltd., States Printers, Jersey.

My father's identity card

Every Friday afternoon he would read to us from classical adventure stories since there were not books for everyone. This was a special treat, and even the big boys listened. We learned to spell as he formed us unto a long line as a spelling bee and asked us how to spell the words we had previously learned from the blackboard. Those who got the spelling right moved up one person. The words were sometimes difficult, such as 'khaki', 'accommodation' and 'dahlia'.

Next to the top class was another room separated by a folding wooden and glass division. In this room the soup, which smelled horrible, was warmed up on a stove which was seldom efficient. There was also another feeble stove in the top class where we gathered sometimes during the lunch hour, and I can remember Piper Van der Vliet pulling out a wobbly tooth for Eileen Farnworth, possibly at her request.

The brightest classroom was the infants` class, which had small desks and the kind teacher was called Miss Luce. She was a pianist and we often heard the charming sound of the little children singing as well as saying their tables out loud.

Towards the end of the war when times were really difficult it was reported by a boy that his lunch had been stolen from his coat which he had left in the boys' lobby. As this had happened before my father put an agile boy into the loft above the lobby with the hatch open together with a chair to aid his descent. This boy had to watch the cloakroom while the other pupils were in class. He saw a very hungry boy from a poor family come into the lobby, take the food and run out of the school grounds. My father was immediately told and he gathered all the boys from the top class who chased the hungry thief into the churchyard, where he was cornered sitting on a gravestone and eating as fast as he could. He never returned to school, and his behaviour showed how very hungry some children had become towards the end of the occupation. I have no doubt that my father would have been distressed to learn of his pupil's hunger.

Our pencils became treasured possessions, and exercise books were used at both ends for different subjects, and only replaced when each full page had been shown to a teacher.

My father organised concerts to entertain the children and sometimes their parents. These consisted of plays and songs he had written, recitations of poetry and prose, and community singing led by the choir. The Constable, Mr Baudains and his wife were present on one occasion and as my father had learned it was their wedding anniversary Eileen Farnworth sang especially for them a song, the words of which were:

Just a song at twilight, when the lights are low,
And the flickering shadows softly come and go.
Though the heart be weary, sad the day and long,
Still to us at twilight comes love's old song,
Comes love's old sweet song.

When she had finished singing the Constable and his wife were in tears.

The stage was constructed by trestle tables, used for the soup kitchen, pushed together and with a chair as a step to climb up. This arrangement was quite perilous and would shake alarmingly, especially when the choir had climbed up and were singing lustily.

My brother had fair hair and blue eyes and was often smiled upon by the soldiers as he possibly looked like their children. One day I had just left the school gates on my way home when I saw him talking to a soldier who was sitting in the hedge outside the Arsenal. The soldier was crying and was showing my brother a photo of some children, who were also fair, and he kept repeating *mein kinder, mein kinder*. Whether my brother reminded him of his children, or that he missed them, or that they had been killed we will never know. As children we had no idea of the horrors of war.

Above: Our Crystal radio set

Below: Pack of cigarettes which arrived on the Vega

10 *Education and the health of the Children: Doctor Likeman*

Following his retirement, one of my father`s treasured possessions was a book entitled *Education and the Second World War*, studies in schooling and social change, edited by Roy Lowe. This book was presented to my father by one of his former pupils, Janet Likeman (*née* Gloyn-Ham). Her contribution to this book was a chapter entitled 'Our dear Channel Islands: a survey of education in Jersey during the German Occupation 1940-45'. Doctor Likeman has very kindly given me permission to copy extracts from her important and thoroughly researched contribution which referred particularly to the Jersey States Intermediate School in St Helier and to the Parish School of St Lawrence.

Doctor Likeman writes:

> St Lawrence Elementary School was the Parish School of St Lawrence. St Lawrence Primary School as it is now called was built in 1901 in the beautiful pink granite characteristic of the Island. In 1940 it was taking children from the ages 6 to 14. It had a playing field and two playgrounds, one for boys and one for girls. It had five classrooms. The headmaster at this time was Mr E.C. Turner who died in September 1940. The new headmaster was Mr H.S. Carter who was transferred from St Luke`s, where he was assistant master. Fortunately he had recently obtained his Brevet de Capacité, a prerequisite for any head teacher in the Island`s elementary schools where the teaching of French continued to be an important part of the

school curriculum.

St Lawrence Elementary and the States` Intermediate had children from the country and town where differences in nutrition and heating occurred. Both head teachers were very committed to the children in their care not only for their physical wellbeing but also to maintain promote and develop their education.

1940 – St. Lawrence Elementary School closed on 29 May for the summer holidays. St. Lawrence is one of the country parishes despite its proximity to St. Helier and the children at this school would be expected to work on the farms, especially as many of their parents were either farmers or farm workers. The school reopened on 2 July after the German Occupation had taken place. The Headmaster, Mr E.C. Turner, was unwell that summer and could not attend all the sessions He died suddenly on 6 September. The Public Instruction Committee appointed Mr H. S. Carter as the new Headmaster. The number of children on the roll at this time was 84. In the Logbook Mr Carter wrote:

"Deeply conscious of my responsibilities it will be my constant endeavour to serve my school and my Parish to the utmost of my ability (23 September 1940)".

This was also the first day the soup arrived from the Chelsea Hotel. Mr Carter faced the problem of heating it and sent for the blacksmith who failed to work out a satisfactory solution. It was finally heated on concrete blocks and a fire basket. Some of the children complained it was slightly sour the next day. In November the sessions started at 10 a.m. to 12.30 p.m. and 2p.m. to 4.15p.m. for infants and 4.30 p.m. for seniors. Mr Carter recorded on 14th November 1940 that attendance was down to 60 this morning due to last night`s gale. M. Marc Ceppi, the French Inspector, continued his inspections of the Elementary Schools throughout the Occupation. On 19 December the children went to the Parish Hall to watch films and returned to school for tea prepared by the staff, the Department of Labour had sent meat paste, cake, jam and sweets. The next afternoon was prize giving, then the holiday.

1941 In January the attendance was 65 per cent due to the cold and snow. In April, the summer term, the hours were 9am to 12 noon and from 1.30p.m. to 4p.m. In May the American Red Cross sent Swiss cheese and two portions were given to each child. On 16 June Mr. Carter recorded that he had received the circular asking if any member of staff could teach German to children willing to learn. He regarded this as unpatriotic and refused to be involved. The Public Instruction Committee decided that the school leaving age should be raised to 15 years to prevent young islanders working for the Germans and the law to this effect was passed on 16 May 1941.

The German Command decided that the rule of the road was to be changed from left to right and Mr Carter had to explain this to the children. Sterling notes and coinage became scarce and Reichmarks became the official currency. Sixteen children wished to learn the German language, of these only six were old enough, and two pupils passed the Intermediate examination. Eighty nine children attended the school. The summer was wet and cold yielding bad harvests and a future detrimental effect on bread rations. The air raid shelter was dug at this time, Miss Laurens retired and the school garden was handed over to the Parish. There was a prize giving but no party at Christmas, Mr Carter described the progress of the school and was congratulated by the Constable, and each child received sweets to the value of one shilling.

1942 School opened on 7 January with 101 children but closed later due to wintry conditions. Medical and dental inspections were carried out with good results. Children were vaccinated against smallpox due to an Island outbreak and many suffered adverse results and the school was closed to allow time for recovery. One pupil developed scarlet fever resulting in the disinfection of the school and one girl gained a free entry into the Intermediate school. Boys over 14 could start their summer holidays on 15 June if they were to be employed in the potato season. The summer was good. Three children and their parents were deported to Germany with the possibility that others would follow. In the road outside signs were erected saying "Schule" and two German Officers inspected the building and asked questions. A team arrived to fit the Jersey shoes in November. These were sabots made at Summerland in Jersey. Eleven men carved 50,000 soles from beech to be attached to uppers. These shoes made a noise in the classrooms and later rubber strips were issued for repairs. At the end of the school year Mr Carter described the events which had taken place, especially the links between home and school and the Constable once again said he had been impressed by the report. There were no prizes but certificates were issued.

1943 Buses ran on charcoal and bicycles were given tyres cut from old car tyres. Children had no protective clothing and it was impossible to dry their clothes in the school. Chicken pox and impetigo were among the illnesses affecting the children in the spring term of 1943. Skin conditions were a problem throughout the Occupation years due to a lack of medical supplies and the lack of soap and hot water for washing. A child in the infants' class developed diphtheria and the other children were sent home for 10 days. Immunisation against diphtheria then followed, and a medical examination showed that the doctor was satisfied with the general health. A sports day was held in the summer term, the boys winning against the girls 40 to 30 points. Another girl won a free scholarship to the Intermediate and the teaching of German became compulsory, the text book was called *Deutsches Leben*. School teachers were asked to attend the German lessons so excluding the possibility of Germans going into classrooms. This was met with a mixed reaction as some felt they were protecting the children by doing so, others refused point blank. Prizes were given to staff and pupils after the scheme had been going for some months, causing embarrassment to some. Mr Carter regarded the teaching of German as unpatriotic and had nothing to do with it. A young teacher, possibly aged about 16 came to the school especially for these sessions. A boy later recalled he had thrown his text book in the water tank above the boys' lavatory as a gesture of disgust and defiance.

So far as I was concerned, I recall that I was not allowed to learn German, but we all knew the German words of *kaput* and *verboten* and some other interesting rude words and my father knew little German apart from the expression *Ich bin eine Jersey man*. (I am a Jersey man). He writes:

> I took no part in these lessons, in fact I absented myself deliberately. After some months I was summoned to College House to report on the progress being made, which I naturally said was excellent. Before I went I thought I had better have a quick look at the exercise books which to my horror were splendidly illustrated by German planes being shot down in flames by Allied aircraft. Fortunately no German ever came to see these works of art.

Doctor Likeman continues:

The new sabot shoes distributed in November were an improvement in some respects but had metal strips which made a clatter. At the end of term in December the children performed two plays with recitations and songs to parents and friends. No prizes and no sweets but each child received half a Reichmark.

1944 This year was one of hope that the Occupation would soon be over, also great anxiety that the islands would have enough food to survive. The sound of battle could be heard in June during the allied landings in Normandy. The island was greatly fortified and the local guns were used against aircraft and ships. It became obvious that the island would not be included in the action and became an island under siege, the Germans were unable to maintain supplies by air and sea so the island had to be self sufficient in food and materials for the occupying forces as well as for the islanders. Due to transport difficulties some children returned to their elementary schools from the Intermediate.

In May 102 children received six ounces of biscuits from the French Secours National. One of the pupils gained a scholarship to Victoria College, the first ever to do so, and another boy to the Intermediate. The summer weather was fine and children recovered from the coughs they had before the holidays. Medical and dental inspections took place and on 19 September Mr. Carter wrote that health generally and bodily development remarkable after four years of occupation. Notification was received that there would be no fuel ration that coming winter so the children gathered wood on the way to school. Head teachers had discretion to close their schools for one or more days if the weather conditions were very wintry. A notice was printed in the Evening Post on the 25th November by the Education Committee as follows:

"The Department of Education are anxious to maintain continuity in school work during the winter, in spite of the difficulties obtaining at present. They feel that the provision of milk and soup to the children outweigh some of these difficulties. The

Department however are fully alive to the defective clothing and footwear which many children are wearing and they will not take proceedings against parents who keep their children at home when the weather is too bad for them to attend school."

The attendance at St. Lawrence remained high. Permission was obtained for four pine trees to be felled providing a supply of wood for classroom fires. An appeal was made for foodstuffs for the poor of St.Helier. At the end of term ceremony Mr. Carter gave a review of the year and the pupils gave a concert before Mr J. Baudains the Constable, the Centenier and parents.

1945 The Medical Officer of Health Dr McKinstry kept a record of the health of the people of Jersey.

Part of his report is as follows:

"The extent to which Jersey has suffered is shown by the fall in the height and weight of schoolchildren, the prevalence of malnutrition amongst the working class in the town, the gross deficiency in shoes and clothing and the increased incidence of lice, impetigo, scabies, ringworm and septic skin conditions.

Due to the severe weather the schools did not open until 8th February and then only for the morning. Soup and milk were distributed to maintain health and every effort was made to maintain the children's education. When afternoon school resumed on 19 March the teaching of German was reintroduced for half an hour three times weekly."

11 Liberation Hopes

Doctor Likeman continues:

> On 7 May the following communication was received by Mr Carter:
>
> "To Head teachers, Department of Education
>
> **4th May 1945** As you know there is a distinct possibility that news may be received shortly of the termination of hostilities. Our local authorities fear that in their joy and excitement some 'hot heads' in the population may cause 'incidents' and that there may be clashes with some of the Occupying Forces. The Department feels that it would be a measure of prudence if parents kept their children at home for a few days to avoid any possible danger. Under the circumstances the Department authorise the head teachers to close the schools for the remainder of the week in which the news is received."

My father then takes up the story in his written memoir:

> On D-Day I was invited to the local doctor's house to hear the official announcement of the Allied landing, alas what dreary months of waiting were still in store for us had we but known. However, this landing had immediate effect on we prisoners in the Channel Islands, for the first thing the Americans did was to erect a powerful radio transmitter in Normandy. Immediately all the deaf aids disappeared from the local cinemas because some ingenious fellow in Jersey discovered it was possible to make the old

fashioned `crystal set` out of odds and ends, and to get a strong signal once a particular spot had been located by the 'cat`s whisker'. I had fortunately obtained both earphones and crystal set and it became necessary to affix an aerial between the chimney stacks of my home. This was successfully accomplished with the passing German soldiery watching my balancing act.

A sense of euphoria spread daily as the news from the battle fronts continued to improve. To this was added the assurance that these islands were surrounded by a chain of allied steel, and that it was no longer possible to be sentenced to imprisonment on the Continent with Belsen as journey's end. The worst that could now happen for committing a 'German' crime was to be sentenced to the local prison. Rumour has it that there was such a lengthy list of prospective inmates that there was at least a six months delay before there was notification of a vacancy. Prisoners were also arranging for their own beds to be installed.

At fixed times of the day I scribbled down the official daily reports from the battle fronts as I listened to my crystal set, and it became apparent that the war in Europe would soon be over. I referred earlier to the ingenuity of the maker of my crystal set. It was approximately treble the size of a matchbox and made of wood with a coil of thin wire inside, no doubt with sufficient turns to match the wavelength of the transmitter. Terminals were fitted at each end for the earth and aerial wires, and a further two for connection to the earphones. In the centre was the screw section of a bicycle valve in which nestled in a bed of silver paper the magic crystal, made so I understand from heating sulphur. Alongside was a moveable arm at the end of which was soldered a piece of thin wire. By careful manipulation of this arm a live spot was found.

German army troops (heer) march past Church Lea on the way to the landing craft; armed British soldiers lead the column

The German Airforce (Luftwaffe) leave beneath our Union Jack

Naval Officers (Kriegsmarine) seem glad to be leaving

Above: German troops enter a landing craft while local people walk around

Left: Local people stand in the wet sand to see the last of the occupying forces depart

12 Liberation Day

My father continues:

On my crystal set a voice could be heard with great clarity on 8th May saying 'the Prime Minister will broadcast to the nation at 3 p.m. to announce the cessation of hostilities'."

I was then living a short distance from the school which I left in sufficient time to be sure my set was working. I took down verbatim the short statement concerning the terms of surrender and the names of the signatories on both sides. Then came the never to be forgotten ending "and our dear Channel Islands will be freed today".

Sadly my wife was ill, but hurrying back to school I took my Union Jack with me. Here was an historic occasion to be celebrated with due pomp and ceremony. The piano was rolled outside, and the children formed up in a hollow square beneath the flagstaff. With considerable emotion I read Winston Churchill's statement of victory in Europe. Miss Luce then seated herself with much trepidation at the piano insisting that I stood between her and the German soldiers, who with guns slung over their shoulders, showed considerable interest in the proceedings.

The singing was rendered with great gusto. First, *Rule Britannia* appropriately stressing 'Britons never shall be slaves', then 'There`ll always be an England, and England shall be free'. Finally, and most important of all, hymn no. 318, the National Anthem, practised each week during the entire Occupation. *God Save the King.* As we sang a senior pupil raised the Union Jack which had been verboten for five years. And the assembly terminated amidst thunderous cheers.

> Thus came our liberation, although no British troops actually landed for over two days due to the intransigence of the local German Commander in refusing to surrender.

There is a copy of my father's handwritten record of Mr Churchill's broadcast. I will never forget that Liberation Day ceremony. It took place outside the Girls' entrance and it took some effort by the older boys to get the old piano down the granite steps in one piece. The flagpole was I think in the shrubbery to the south, and I think the soldiers were standing just in front of this.

Part of Doctor Likeman`s final account reads as follows:

> HMS *Beagle* sailed around Noirmont and anchored in St. Aubin`s Bay at 10.00 a.m. The unconditional surrender of the German forces was accepted by Major General Snow. As the British forces landed and advanced through the ecstatic crowds they threw sweets and chocolates to the Islanders. So precious was this extra addition for many of them that it was taken home and Liberation supper that night included for some families a careful division of a bar of chocolate. Other families brought out special items that had been saved especially for this very special day. Other Islanders revealed cars that had been hidden for five years, and somehow petrol was found. Union Jacks flew everywhere. The celebrations went on for days, with as many people as possible gathering in St. Helier to celebrate their freedom. The children were not at school.

So ends the invaluable contribution by Doctor Likeman to the history of education at St Lawrence Elementary School during the Occupation.

I went with my father to see the arrival of the liberating soldiers and saw them on the balcony at the Pomme d'Or Hotel and the raising of the flag, but little else as I was too short. It took a while to understand what had actually happened.

The school was selected as the centre for the collection of all German military personnel prior to their shipment to England, and so that they could be deloused. This was an interesting time for children since the soldiers threw into the hedges as they waited in the roads various personal possessions including knives and cameras which they knew would be confiscated, and which the children enjoyed collecting. I found a good camera.

I went with my father to see the German troops leaving the Island. I saw the landing craft in St Aubin's Bay drawn up on the beach to the west of the old swimming pool. It was low tide. The stern doors were wide open and the troops were in long lines waiting to go on board, watched by some of the civilian population. The troops looked undisciplined and untidy but very pleased to be going home, quite different from the days when they would march past singing aye ee aye oh aye oh, or doing the goosestep.

Liberation, May 1945. The three of us on the wall at Church Lea with the Union Jack flying. The chimney held the aerial for the crystal set

13 The Parish Hall

The Parish Hall or *Salle Paroissale* was built in 1882 when Clement Le Gros was Constable. It is another fine granite building to the south of the Arsenal. There is a memorial stone on the east side of the Hall commemorating those who lost their lives during the wars of 1914 to 1918 and 1939 to 1945. There is now also a stone dedicated to the memory of the militia men of the St Lawrence Battalian who lost their lives in the Battle of Jersey on the 6th January 1781.

During the Occupation the Parish Hall was the centre of the Parish affairs. The Constable and Centeniers were greatly respected, and I never saw a uniformed policeman during the Occupation years. As mentioned previously in my father's memoirs, it was the ARP (Air Raid Precautions) centre before the Occupation began.

Towards the end of the Occupation it became a centre for raising funds for the International Red Cross which supplied us with life saving food parcels which were brought to the Island by the SS *Vega*.

My father writes:

> The Entertainments Committee of St Lawrence`s Football Club arranged a monthly stage show in the Parish Hall during the later months of the Occupation. The ingenuity of the inhabitants was once again exemplified, for each concert had to be specially written and submitted to the German censor – as for lighting effects, car batteries were used. These live shows

were great boosters to morale, and are still talked about. A copy of the front page of one programme reads:

> "St Lawrence Parish Hall, by kind permission of the Constable, the Entertainment Section of St Lawrence F.C. present 'GO AS YOU PLEASE' A Competition for Residents and Natives of St Lawrence. Profits in aid of The Constable`s Charity Fund and St Lawrence F.C. Saturday, April 22nd 1944 at 6 p.m. prompt".

There is a list of the Officers of St Lawrence F.C.
I have recently come across the words of a ditty written by myself sung by the entire company to the tune of There is a tavern in the town:

"My fuel ration is so small (is so small)
One hundred weight between us all (tween us all)
The logs are wet, as wet as can be
It would be dear if it was free!
///Chorus: Fare thee well for we are going
For to do a spot of sawing
And of chopping and of lopping of a tree (a tree)
Who owns the tree we do not know (do not know)
And we have permit none to show (none to show)
We`ll take our truck, and hope with luck
To get some wood in time for tea (time for tea)
///CHORUS///
Now for some paper and a light (and a light)
Yes, everything is getting tight (very tight)
Except the clothes you`re wearing on your back
Which are in fact extremely slack (oh so slack)
///Chorus///
And then you have to blow and blow (blow and blow)
That dratted fire will not go (will not go)

St. Lawrence Parish Hall.

(By kind permission of the Constable).

The Entertainment Section of St. Lawrence F.C.

PRESENT

'GO AS YOU PLEASE'

A Competition for

Residents and Natives of St. Lawrence.

Profits in aid of The Constable's Charity Fund
and St. Lawrence F. C.

SATURDAY, APRIL 22nd, 1944,

AT 6 P.M. PROMPT.

The bellows puff and so do you
Until your face in hue is blue (hue is blue)
///Chorus///
You`d think our spirit would be broke (would be broke)
Living thus beneath the Nazi yoke (Nazi yoke)
In point of fact the contrary is true
Our spirit`s still red white and blue (far from blue)
///Chorus///"

I don't know how that last verse passed the Censor maybe it was not included for submission. I have a document kept by my father from the States of Jersey Department of Labour dated 11th November 1944 giving him permission to fell and (or) cut up two trees for his own personal use at Les Vaux, St Lawrence, the consent of the proprietor had to be obtained before any work could be carried out under a 'Forestry' permit.

I recall another song my father wrote, to the tune of *The Quartermaster's Stores*, with additions in Jersey French:

"There was Klim, Klim, no longer you'll be slim
Dans la Bouete, dans la bouete
There was Klim, Klim, no longer you`ll be slim
Dans la Red Cross Cardboard bouete.
There was Spam, Spam, better than any ham
Dans la Bouete, etc.
There were fags, fags, good for all the lads
Dans la bouete etc.

Klim was dried milk, spelled backwards, and la bouete is Jersey French for box.

I also found a poem written by my father on the back of a postcard which was probably recited at one of the concerts:

"Counsel to all

"Gather ye limpets for your meal
The tide is quickly rising.
Unless you do you`ll surely feel
A void, most agonising.
This glorious state in which we live
The worse it is a getting
No eats, no clothes, coal dust to sieve
For kith and kin we`re fretting
We thought it bad right at the first
When youth and blood were warmer
But stores are spent, the worse, the worst
Times still succeed the former
Then not be coy but use your time
To buy or scrounge or barter
Unless you chase up every `line`
You`ll soon be in hereafter."

(after Robert Herrick 1591-1674, with apologies)

Then, as liberation approached, my father wrote the following:

"Happy days will soon be here
The end of misery and fear
We`ll soon be in the mood to cheer
Happy days will soon be here.
You men will soon have plenty fags
You women will forget to nag
When overhead there flies that flat
Happy days will soon be here."

My mother was deaf, and we therefore had to sit right in the front of the rows of benches at these concerts. Unfortunately my family was afflicted by untimely giggles and sniggers when the performance on the stage became too awful, and I remember her pushing my brother under the bench as he was laughing so much at the screeching voice of a very wobbly soprano. He was very small.

My father kept an exercise book, which I still have, in which he glued cuttings about the *Vega*, the ship bringing the parcels to us and in particular a cutting from the *Evening Post* dated Friday December 8 1944 which reads:

> "Red Cross Supplies on the way. I am officially informed by the German Military Authorities that a Red Cross ship was, weather permitting, due to leave Lisbon on on Thursday, December 7th, for the Channel Islands. The ship will call at Guernsey first, en route for Jersey.
>
> A.M. Coutanche, Bailiff."

A further and very important message from the Bailiff, dated 3rd January 1945 and printed in the *Evening Post* reads as follows:

> "MESSAGE FROM THE BAILIFF TO THE PEOPLE OF JERSEY
>
> After long and difficult negotiations the International Red Cross has sent to the Channel Islands the ss. *Vega*, carrying special delegates and valuable gifts from the British, Canadian and New Zealand Red Cross Societies, consisting of medical supplies, food parcels, soap, salt and tobacco.
>
> A special gift of layettes comes to us from Lady Campbell, the wife of the British Ambassador in Lisbon. Important conferences, which I was privileged to attend, have taken place in Guernsey, and are now taking place in Jersey, in order that the Insular Governments, by exchange of views

with the Occupying Authorities, and with the delegates, may ascertain the ways and means by which the shipping available for the purpose may best be used to relieve the most urgent needs of the Channel Islands and in order that proposals for further relief may, through the delegates, be made known to the International Red Cross.

In Jersey, as in Guernsey, the Insular Representatives of the joint Red Cross and St John Organizations, together with the Medical Officer of Health, are attending the conferences, and in Jersey we have the advantage of the presence of Doctor Drécourt, representative of the French Red Cross.

Arrangements, in which the Constables and, through them, the farmers, and in which the wholesale grocers and, through them, the retailers play an important part, were worked out before my departure for Guernsey, in order to ensure a speedy, efficient and absolutely impartial distribution among the entire civil population. The delegates, on arrival in Jersey, handed over the cargo to me, on behalf of the Island, and distribution will take place at the earliest possible moment in accordance with the pre-arranged plan. Details are being published in the Press as to the means by which every inhabitant may receive his or her parcel. The transport is being provided by volunteers. The distribution is being carried out as a free and voluntary service. Every inhabitant is entitled to receive his or her parcel as an absolute free gift from the Red Cross.

I hear expressed on every side the desire to contribute to a Red Cross Fund. It may not be possible for any transfer of money to be made until the end of the war; but a Red Cross Fund is now open. I know from my conversation with them that the delegates will carry away with them a happy impression of this wish of the Channel Islands (for similar steps are being taken in Guernsey) to show their appreciation of the wonderful work of their Friend in Need – the Red Cross.

It is thought that the parcels carried in the ss. *Vega* may be just sufficient for two distributions, but it is the urgent advice of the delegates that a second distribution should not take place until we know when the Vega may again be expected in Channel Island waters and we are aware of the nature of the next cargo.

It is obvious that valuable as the food parcels are, we require many other additional commodities if a reasonable standard of life is to be maintained especially now that stocks of food, including flour and potatoes, under the control of the Insular Government, are nearly exhausted.

I appeal to every member of the community to treat his or her parcel as an 'non-ration' and to make it last as long as possible. Another distribution will be made as soon as it is prudent to do so; but no promise can be given as to when that will be.

Plans will be worked out immediately for the distribution of the soap, tobacco and layettes.

No regulations enforceable in a Court of Law are being made in Jersey with regard to the distribution of these Red Cross gifts, but I ask the people of Jersey to regard it as a condition of honour that no person shall sell his or her parcel in whole or in part and that no person shall seek to obtain, by any means whatever, more than his or her fair share of any Red Cross gift.

I believe that the will of the people will demand that any person who fails to observe this condition of honour shall be debarred from receiving any share of future Red Cross gifts.

A.M Coutanche, Bailiff"

This revealing message from the Bailiff must have given great hope to the Islanders struggling to feed themselves and their families. I believe my parents were often hungry and lost weight, but they always made sure we were fed as well as it was possible. I can just remember the Red Cross boxes on our dining room table, and that we stared at the contents unable to believe our eyes.

It was in the Parish Hall that I learned about the true horrors of the war. We were still living at Church Lea and waiting for Windycroft to be repaired when my father took me to see some films which were to be shown there, and unbeknown to him one of these films was I think a Pathé News item showing the first terrible pictures of a Nazi Concentration Camp. I remember the feeling of shock and horror and absolute silence in the hall as no one could believe what they were seeing, and the sight of the emaciated skeletons of the living and piles of naked dead is still with me. When we got home I cried for a long time, and when my father came to comfort me I remember saying to him that I would never understand how people could behave like this to other human beings. I then realised how fortunate we had been.

14 The Parish Church of St Lawrence

This ancient and beautiful church, the church of St Lawrence the Martyr who, according to legend, was burned to death on a grid iron, was according to a historical document consecrated on 4th January 1199. The Parish cannon was kept in the nave and a large doorway now blocked up in the west wall was used to move it in and out. The church yard was a good source of interest for us with its lovely headstones, particularly in the south west corner, also the gargoyles on the north side. We would hang about at dusk sometimes, before curfew, and hope to see ghosts rising from their graves.

At one time I sang in the choir. I doubt whether we wore robes, but I recall processing around the church singing the first hymn. During the winter the church was like ice as of course there was no heating, and the exhaled breaths of the choir hung like a cloud above us. After a lengthy sermon it was difficult to stand up as it was so cold. I remember being in the choir stalls at a funeral, the first I ever attended, staring at the coffin, wondering what was inside.

At that time some ancient flags hung near the altar on the south side and I remember wishing I could see them properly. These I have recently discovered were the regimental flags of the Royal Jersey Militia. During the Battle of Jersey two St. Lawrence men were killed and six wounded, and there is a stained glass window in memory of this.

I attended lessons to prepare for Confirmation but was asked to leave the class by the Rector as instead of reciting the Collect for the day I could not stop laughing at a spider walking around his shoulders.

Sometimes the Verger accidentally left the small door on the north side unlocked which led on to dusty, narrow winding granite stairs and into the belfry where the huge bell hung, and which we climbed whenever we could. We did not stay long as we were anxious not to be locked in, or to be found where we should not have been, but if we were in the churchyard we always checked the door to see if we could get in.

The bell rang out over the Parish on Liberation Day, and a service of thanksgiving was held.

15 *Afterwards*

Once the German soldiers had been fumigated and disarmed at the School they marched past our house and down to St Aubin's Bay where they were shipped to England to be repatriated. I can remember that the soldiers were very cheerful as they went past, happy the war was over and they would be going home. We watched them go, and they often waved.

This was a wonderful time for us. We were a gang of children of various ages and we roamed the Parish and investigated the German camps and huts, gun emplacements and bunkers. Since we knew about the underground hospital (now Jersey War Tunnels) one day we walked down Ville Emphrie and up towards the main entrance. However from past reconnaissance we knew the doors would be locked but that there was another escape entrance in the land above the hospital. We found this again and using a saucer of melted candlewax holding a rag which was ignited with a match we descended the long concrete steps to see what was below. It was very frightening as we could hear water dripping and echoes of strange sounds, like people calling out. Holding on to each other in the near total darkness we got as far as one of the wards equipped with beds which we could barely see in the dim light, then we fled.

There was quite a delay in our return to Windycroft as it had been used as a barracks by the German soldiers and was in a poor condition. It needed painting throughout, the staircase was worn away by jackboots and there was a stove in every room which had a chimney. There was a gun emplacement in the field covered by camouflage netting and several interesting bunkers, one to the north east of the house, one in the lane and another in the field to the south west. There were slit trenches all along the west side of the house and garden. Once we were re-established my father filled these in together with our old air raid shelter and began to dig his garden. For a while the house smelled of what was thought to be the cleaner used for the soldiers' weapons, and somehow it took time for the house to get rid of the rather ghostly feeling of its previous occupants.

Stories began to circulate about how the occupying forces had been outwitted by the locals. My father recalls one of these in his memoirs, as told to him by his friend the local Undertaker:

> "Once the pig had been slaughtered the carcass was strung up. The panic started early the next morning, when the cowman came rushing back to say the farm next door was being searched for hidden stores. I shouted to my mother to get me one of our best sheets, into which we quickly bundled the corpse. With some difficulty we carried it across the yard to where the coffins were stored. In no time we had the

pig installed and screwed down, and we were just breathing a huge sigh of relief when the search party entered. After a thorough search in which they found half a bag of wheat, which was confiscated, they departed well satisfied. I decided to get rid of this incriminating evidence as quickly as possible, and being unable to contact my uncle who owned the pig I decided to make a personal delivery. Being an undertaker, and it being necessary to deliver the coffins to my various clients, I had acquired a pony and carriage. These were prepared, and the loaded coffin covered with a tarpaulin. It appeared that luck favoured the brave, and all went well until as I approached Hautes Croix I was confronted by a road block with a search by the soldiers for black market goods being meticulously carried out. It was indicated that I should dismount and expose my load. When the covering was removed I indicated the coffin contained a body by lifting one end, and saying kaput, kaput!` and holding my nose. Without hesitation they indicated I could drive on, and being good Roman Catholics crossed themselves. The delivery was made without further incident, and I collected the coffin some weeks later, this time for a human corpse."

My father had previously mentioned in his writings of a Lieutenant Zievecka (?) of Hamburg who told my father he would end up working at the Pomme D'Or Hotel. As a postscript to his notes written in the old exercise book on 20th June 1941, and copied at the beginning of this account, on the back cover of this book, he writes:

Postscript (forty years later) – I was successful in passing the Brevet de Capacité, in those days an essential qualification for a headship, and within weeks I was appointed as head of St Lawrence School. It was particularly gratifying to me that this building should have been selected as the centre for the collection of all German military personnel, prior to their shipment to England. The wheel had come a full circle, and the prediction of a German officer that I would find myself washing dishes at the Pomme d'Or for the Nazi Strength through Joy movement fortunately proved false.

Although we did not know of this at the time, we were saved by the decision by the Allied Forces Command not to bomb and invade Jersey and the other Channel Islands.

This collection of memories is a tribute to my parents. I know how fortunate my sister, brother and I were, not only to have lived during a time of such history, but also to have had a mother and father who did everything possible to get us through it, and who always put our care before everything else.